HOME
IS WHERE
THE BARN IS

HELEN ALLEN BURCHELL

Copyright © 2024 Helen Allen Burchell
All rights reserved
First Edition

Fulton Books
Meadville, PA

Published by Fulton Books 2024

ISBN 979-8-88982-883-9 (paperback)
ISBN 979-8-88982-884-6 (digital)

Printed in the United States of America

In memory of Davanna Sun King, my "Grand Foal,"
and in honor of Dollar and Skye, who have refilled
my barn and my heart with unimaginable joy

The Grandest Foal
(Author Unknown)

I'll lend you for a little while,
my grandest foal, God said.
For you to love while he's alive,
and mourn for when he's dead.
It may be one or twenty years,
or days or months, you see.
But will you til I take him back,
Take care of him for me?
He'll bring his charms to gladden you
and should his stay be brief,
you'll have those treasured memories,
as solace for your grief.
I cannot promise he will stay,
since all from earth return.
But there are lessons taught on earth
I want this foal to learn.
I've looked the wide world over
in my search for teachers true.
and from the throngs that crowd life's lanes,
with trust, I have selected you.
Now will you give him all your love?
Nor think the labor vain.
Nor hate me when I come
to take him back again?
I know you'll give him tenderness
and love will bloom each day.
And for the happiness you've known,
you will forever-grateful stay.
But should I come and call for him
much sooner than you'd planned,
you'll brave the bitter grief that comes,
and maybe understand.

CONTENTS

Acknowledgments vii

Chapter 1:   The Shocking Evolution of Horse Care 1
Chapter 2:   Pasture Features of a Small Turnout Area 5
Chapter 3:   Stall Basics and Maintenance 9
Chapter 4:   The Barn Elements 14
Chapter 5:   Water 19
Chapter 6:   Feeding the Complex Equine Digestive System 23
Chapter 7:   Grooming and Skin Care 29
Chapter 8:   Skin Diseases 35
Chapter 9:   Characteristics of the Hoof 39
Chapter 10: Dollar's Crisis: Facing Mortality 45
Chapter 11: Blankets and Halters: The Debate 49
Chapter 12: Afterthoughts of Dreams and Memories 53
             Recommended Product Lists 54

Works Cited 65

ACKNOWLEDGMENTS

To Michael, who has willingly shared me with the horses his entire life and who very wisely noted, "You won't let me have a four-wheeler, but you put me on a thousand-pound horse to ride through the woods!" To which I replied, using my maternal logic on safety, "But son, a horse has a brain!" We have a lifetime of trail-riding, stall-cleaning, hay-hauling, and barn-building memories. Thank you, Michael, for continuing to offer to help at the barn every time you are home and the interest you have shown in me as I have pursued this passion.

To Curtis, who has been my partner in the second phase of horse ownership. You have given me your full support in this venture and conveniently shared that you had always wanted horses. Your connection to Eddie Tuck resulted in the gift of the two walking horses we happily share. You have spent untold hours reworking the barn and maintaining the pasture. You have never questioned the need to help me finance this venture in the form of veterinarian and farrier expenses. Thank you too for always understanding that even after a long day, the horses' feeding schedule still takes precedence over ours. I am eternally grateful.

Dr. Paul Erwin and recently *Dr. Natalie Barker* of Chatham Animal Hospital have proven to be the most dependable and most knowledgeable veterinarians one could imagine. I am so fortunate to have them close and hope they know how highly regarded they are in this area. I owe you a lifetime of appreciation for Dollar's recovery.

Eddie and Craig Martin of Roxboro are a rare find in the farrier business. They have a huge clientele, many with large barns, yet they are just as attentive and reliable in the scheduling of our two horses that are a county away from their home. Thank you for your work in attending to our horse during his laminitis bout.

Thank you to *Southern States* of Danville, Virginia, for your reliable Nutrena horse feed products and your willingness to order whatever your horse customers need.

To Danny Slade, who has driven from Burlington to deliver excellent quality hay to us for over twenty-five years, thank you. I literally could not have horses here without you.

To Pat Owen who along with *Scott and Robyn* encouraged me to actually write this book. Thank you for patiently listening to me drone on and on about horses and horse issues. Your willingness to always assist me with technical issues has been an enormous help and has given me the courage to tackle this project. Thank you for volunteering your remarkable photography skills to illustrate this work. You have been the most loyal friend one could ask for.

Finally, to all my horses—past and present—I hope you know how much you are loved and how proud you have made me all these years.

CHAPTER 1

The Shocking Evolution of Horse Care

In the beginning…Michael and Dixie

You have noticed it and have probably acknowledged it as time has passed, all our domesticated dogs and cats seem inclined to get diseases once only attributed to humans. The feeling that pets are more needy, more expensive to keep, and more time-consuming is quite prevalent. It is likely that domestic animals were always that way, but their owners were not informed and more prone to doing things in the "old" way. Those old ways of maintaining domesticated animals have been impacted, in part, by the increasing proximity of those animals to humans in urban and city settings, as well as advances in veterinary medicine.

Horses, too, seem more sensitive to environmental issues today and require much more diligent care than years ago. Today's horse management is radically different from the years of my childhood when my passion for horses took over. When I recall dusty feed rooms filled floor to ceiling with bushels of corn kernels or oats and only a shovel to use as a measuring guide, I am filled with dread wondering how much harm might have resulted in later years. As I recall, all those horses thrived, however, and seemed to rarely need a vet, or shots, and certainly not regular visits from the area blacksmith. Amazingly, these lax measures seemed adequate to sustain our equine charges from our childhood years through our college semesters.

It was quite common then—no worries about West Nile virus, Coggins test, or flu vaccines. If a horse pasture had a creek as a water source, no one gave that a second thought. We spent more time riding than hauling water or cleaning stalls. There were no creature comforts such as barn fans or wash stalls. Amazingly, fence feeders were the norm, and only the horses' predetermined pecking order determined which horses ate well. Supplements occasionally came in the form of a trailer load of dried corn stalks from a neighbor's garden or bags of grass clippings pitched over the fence. Mercifully, we never had any colic, ulcers, or Cushings cases equal to what horse owners experience today.

Fly masks or fly sheets did not exist, and no one had "fly spray." Summer trail riding was miserable, and low-hanging limbs provided the branches we broke off and carried to whisk biting flies from horse and rider. Worming was "hit or miss." There were rumors of some type of tube-worming, but the old-timers swore by the chewed tobacco wad method fed by hand to horses and mules, followed by a swig from a Coke bottle. (You may rightly assume that there was also no consideration paid to whether the first frost had occurred prior to this process. This is a reference to the targeted eradication of the botfly worm eggs that is best accomplished in the colder autumn temperatures.) Additionally, no one ever concerned themselves with any hay analysis and the feed adjustments that would have revealed. Most only followed the basic rules of feeding: feed on time, never switch feed suddenly, and keep your feed room locked for those that might break in and overeat.

(Note: While it is true that the chewed tobacco wad wormer method was crude by our standards, it has been determined that the nicotine in tobacco can be moderately effective in eradicating worms in horses.)

Without any awareness, the misery index of horses and the lack of knowledge by horsemen was high in numerous other areas as well. Some locals fed unsold loaves of bread from the nearby Merita bakery outlet with no fear or knowledge of future insulin resistance and carb overloading consequences. Most large farm pastures included an apple tree or two with bushels of brown fragrant fruit there for the horses' pleasure. Most of these pastures included another permanent hazard. Fences were barbed or electric, and there was always one horse "Houdini" who could come and go as they pleased. These characters bore lifelong scars. It was rare to ever see a solid-colored bay or chestnut without a myriad of white hair areas that had healed over as a result of some unexplained fence accident. Saddle sores or rubbing up against an exposed nail or two would cause the same unsightly white spots long before anyone thought about the benefits of a correctly fitted saddle or horse-proofing a stall. Funny, even as long as medicine cabinets have contained Vaseline ointment, no one thought to use it on horses to prevent the white hair from growing in.

(Note: If electric fencing is your only option, know that most horses will run through it unless they were raised in that type of fence. Mares will teach babies a lifelong respect for it.)

Those babies grew up in rough stalls that had chewed wood from a generation of previous cribbers or bored horses that devoured their wallboards like voracious beavers. Apparently, many horses lived with the secret of their wood addiction and thrived on it.

Those resilient young horses that found their way into our barns were sacked out, saddled, lounged occasionally, and ridden in round pens and plowed fields. Their training was about as far removed from dressage as possible. It did work for our purposes, and later, these same horses would be trail horses in training. The most important factor to success and survival was the use of an additional seasoned horse to "pony" with the young ones. Let me be clear. Training was either "breaking" (away from home and out of sight) or "gentling," and the lines were too blurred for the novice horse owner to feel that any new horse was reliable. It was my experience that neither of these two methods of training ever eliminated the barn sour horse who would not willingly ride away from the barn, or the ones that wanted to race back to the stable when the trail turned toward home. Though demoralizing, those behaviors did not ruin the experience for those of us in the "horse crazy" category.

Instead, it did reinforce the adage that "the horse you get on is not the same horse you get off." Translation: Every time we rode, we were made aware that we were schooling for better or worse—no matter whether the discipline being employed was English or Western.

There was a way to separate the horses by really concerning characteristics. This remains true, and the serious rider should remember: "A bad horse will hurt you. A crazy horse will hurt himself in order to hurt you." There is hope for the former, but not the latter. Bucking under saddle was always acceptable early on, but rearing was, and is, a really bad sign and almost impossible to remedy. Most other negative interactions with our horses are due to us not being patient, consistent, and being clear in our demands. Those guidelines will never change. As a result, current training methods are carried out more slowly with better long-lasting results.

Hopefully, with these reminders, we can appreciate the degree to which horse care has become more refined, more purposeful, and more consistent with science. A good part of this management evolution, in many instances, including mine, is based on logistics. More horses are kept on small farms that allow more frequent interaction between horses and owners. While positive in most aspects, this arrangement requires more planning and care than the more independent horse ownership situations of the past that were described earlier. This treatment of successful horse management is a compilation of old tried and true measures that should make a seamless transition for today's novice horse enthusiast and his ever-evolving equine companions' needs under more modern circumstances.

CHAPTER 2

Pasture Features of a Small Turnout Area

*A horse loves freedom, and the
weariest horse will roll or break
into a gallop when he is turned loose in the open.*

—G. Raftery

Any random Google search will detail the ideal ratio of horses to acreage; most recommend two-plus acres for two horses. While that is the usual measure, these figures are twice as much land as we have ever owned. Before being skeptical, consider the advantages we gain in our limited situation. My pasture area is divided into four cross-fenced areas. The gated entryway to the barn allows access to hay trailers, vets, and dump trucks delivering sawdust and rock. When not in use, this area is a small, shady turnout area with another gated access to a level riding ring with a river sand and rock-dust surface that we drag and maintain weekly. The riding ring area's surface holds up in all weather in that it provides safe footing following extended periods of rain or snow. The rest of the turnout area is cross-fenced and gated into two other grassy lots.

In this limited area situation, the horses and the entire outdoor area are visible to me from the house at all times. Even at night, floodlights illuminate the entire outdoor area. Visibility is the safety feature that we appreciate the most about our limited acreage.

In terms of visibility, imagine the reassurance of being able to walk over, mow, or weedeat every foot of the area your horses use as pasture. The necessity to manage the plants in your pasture cannot be overstated. Unwanted weeds and undergrowth can be removed quickly. Pay attention to any extra tall, broad-leaved grasses that can cause eye infections. Oak leaves, acorns, maple, and cherry trees are common here and seem to accumulate or sprout up overnight, causing an immediate toxic threat to horses. In general, it is the withered leaves in autumn that pose the greatest risk of colic and laminitis when ingested. (Our vets have confirmed that their overall cases of toxicity-related calls are elevated every fall.)

One plant in particular, American pokeweed (or poke sallet and poke salat), incorrectly pronounced and spelled as "salad," merits more thorough consideration. This is an imposing plant, growing four to ten feet in height. It has simple nondescript green leaves on green to reddish-purple stems with purple berries at maturity. It is necessary to highlight the toxicity of this plant for horses because it is so common in the US. The young green leaves are considered a staple in Appalachia and other areas of the deep south. For this reason, many erroneously consider pokeweed to be innocuous and underestimate the need to remove it from pastures. (Interestingly, its latent toxicity did meet a medical need among the poor generations of people in the past. It was used as a vermifuge [worm purger] in humans.)

Again, these small lots unquestionably provide us with an upper hand with regard to routine health emergencies that large landowners might encounter more frequently. Fencing, as referenced before, is an important consideration. The best option is a traditional four-board structure made of pressurized lumber. (Never use "treated wood," which is coated in a salty brine that encourages the terrible habit of chewing.) The boards should be no less than one-by-six in lengths of eight feet. The gap spacing should prevent the possibility of horses pushing under and between the boards. The top board should be at the height of the horse' upper throat to discourage the action of pushing over. It is widely advised to top the entire length of fence with a heavy gauge hot wire. Know that most horses can sense and hear the pulse of electricity so that it is not a real threat to them, and the wire can eventually be turned off completely. The wire also helps to discourage that old wood-chewing habit. (*Note: An experienced fence installer will use round vertical posts to support the flat boards. It is a trade secret that when square posts shift, it throws off the alignment of the boards.*)

The last word on barbed wire is this—it is inhumane and should never be used. Horses that get entangled have been known to struggle to the death to free themselves. Oddly enough, it is said that mules will stand and patiently wait to be freed in such circumstances. Know that, tragically, horses never will.

Your fence is only as reliable as your gate system. They are so important that they are the focus of the number 1 rule of any farm: "Leave all gates the way you find them when you pass through." That admonishment relates to the open or shut position of the gate and the latching mechanism. No excuses or any circumstances override this imperative. There is the potential of heavy litigation regarding fault in this matter with regard to livestock on the loose. Dependable gates are readily available and come in standard sizes, with round horizontal bars. They can, however, be installed incorrectly without proper consideration. The narrowest bar gaps are to be set at the bottom of the gate so that it is harder to wedge a hoof between the bars. The side hinge bolts have to be correctly aligned (down turned at the top, upright at the bottom) to prevent the gate from being lifted up by a horse's head. (This is related to the warning that you should never tie a horse to a gate or anything else that is unstable.) Your gate will come with a chain latch, but it is advisable to install a second security mechanism. All gates and doors at my barn have latch redundancy. Trust me, if you ever experience chasing a horse down the road at night with a flashlight, in traffic, alone, you will appreciate the security of a double lock.

On that note, horses will paw, pull, bump, push, rub, and bite on anything that moves and makes noise until they master it or tear it down. It is always best to "snug up" chains and clasps as close as possible. In a related observation, it is 100 percent predictable that if you do any work or install something new in any area to which they have free access, they will immediately go to that spot to closely examine and usually undo your work. Enough situations like those noted above and you should be well on your way to knowing why it is s so important for you to start "thinking like a horse," which, I might add, is half the battle.

CHAPTER 3

Stall Basics and Maintenance

Care, and not fine stables, makes a good horse.

—Danish proverb

It all started here with a two-stall, tin-covered shed. Overtime, two more stalls, a tack room, and a hay room were added. More recently, a run-in shed and a wash stall were connected. Originally, our stall size was a little less than the recommended twelve-by-twelve-foot measure. After all, our Arabians were only 15.2, and they were outside most of the time, so the situation was appropriate. Fortunately, the dividing walls were set in a wood channel, and removing them was a simple task. Our new Tennessee walking horses measure seventeen hands so, now, out of necessity, we have two large fifteen-by-twelve stalls. This extra space makes a positive difference in all the desirable elements of a confined space. The horses are content enough to lie down and rest. They are easier to groom, and their stalls are easier to clean than was always the case in a smaller stall.

The flooring combination consists of stall mats over no. 57 gravel. Our bedding of choice is sawdust—not shavings. We have used both, but the shavings lack absorbency and cannot be strained through the rake tines. While ideal for a birthing stall or temporary show stalls, the shavings are just not cost-efficient for my operation. There are many new options for bedding, though some old types still are in use, such as peanut hulls and shredded newspaper. (This discussion reminds me that the desperation of the American Plains Indians led them to pack dried "buffalo chips" around their babies inside their cradle boards to keep them dry and comfortable.) While we might assume that buffalo chips are not ever going to be a popular option for stall, it is possible that other desperate horse owners might have tried those also. You are most likely going to choose a type that is the most available, easy to store, and reasonably priced. Whatever you choose, make sure it is something that horses will not eat.

Cleaning or picking out stalls is best done in the morning while the horses are turned out. This schedule allows adequate time for the bedding to dry out completely before the horses are brought in for the night. You need two rakes for this chore; the first is a yard rake for skimming over the footfalls to level out and bank the bedding up against the walls. (The leveling is not only aesthetically pleasing but is necessary to offset back problems in horses that stand too long in stalls with uneven footing.) Banking the bedding against the walls has two purposes:

1. Horses are less likely to get cast in the stall if they lay down and have to roll upward toward the wall.
2. The banked-up bedding is more likely to remain dry for use when the coverage gets low.

The second rake is the manure fork that is used to carefully pick up and strain out the manure for takeaway. This daily process is an opportunity for the horseman to assess any notable changes—either in frequency, amount, color, or consistency of droppings. (Any of which would be concerning.) (*Note: Stallions and geldings usually prefer to soil the middle of their stalls, while mares prefer the area next to a wall. While all horses are different, you will want to keep this pattern in mind when locating feeders, water, and servings of hay.*)

Rake down and pull out as much wet material as possible; the ammonia from urine is more detrimental to the hygiene of a stall than manure. The ammonia is very irritating to a horse's eyes and nose overtime. (Feeding grain containing too much protein will make the urine even more potent. If you are the one cleaning stalls, this condition will be hard for you to ignore when in close proximity to the odor.) The final step is just a personal preference. It really looks like a professional job if you rake your way out of the stall.

Unbelievably, there were some racehorses that were trained to relieve themselves on cue so as to take care of business before a race. (It was accomplished by the handler's whistling, which was started when foals were observed in the process.) This particular method could also eliminate the ammonia buildup referenced above. The incident that was related to me was in regard to a stallion who, being trained in this way, was regularly turned out and then prompted to "go." All this worked well until the owners hired help to feed for a long weekend and forgot to tell them to take the stallion out. Needless to say, the horse (who was a good boy) did not urinate for over two days and was not left alone inside again.

For those of us whose horses are not so well-trained or considerate, the daily chore of "mucking out," or "picking out," stalls is a constant. The term "cleaning" more accurately involves removing all of the bedding periodically, down to the mats. (European horsemen do not understand the American need to be so diligent about stall cleaning. They choose, during their cold winters, to let the straw and manure [which gives off heat] to build up. They justify their methods by comparing their stall bedding to a mattress-like surface, while our stall surface is more like a thin sheet on the floor.) At least we avoid their Herculean task of spring stall cleaning that usually involves several days, a hearty crew with shovels, mattocks, and a backhoe. We might give these Europeans a pass when we realize, in some areas, their horses are basically forced to winter over inside during their extended brutally cold seasons.

The amount of sawdust needed to adequately bed the stall will vary by horse. But in general, you should start with four or five inches. A good test is to be aware if you can feel the mats under your feet; if that is the case, add more. When removing manure, be as conservative as possible with the bedding material. Leave any bedding that retains absorbency properties and any leftover hay. If you start with a good base and are careful, you probably will not need to re-bed the stalls more than once a week, depending on the weather and individual circumstances.

Corner feeders are safe and secure for grain. Again, place these at an appropriate height away from manure areas. (Your water buckets should also be on another wall to prevent grain droppings that sour the water.) After installing the feeders, use a small bit to drill down, forming three holes to allow water to drain when you need to wash out the feeders.

Two five-gallon flat-back buckets per stall are the best for water. (Larger ones are too hard to manage, and it is best to ensure a continued supply with two buckets in the event that one is pushed down.) The standard-colored bucket that is most readily available has two black rubber pieces over the edges of the metal handles. Our horses chew those off immediately. It is very dangerous to leave those ends exposed. The bare hooks can rip a nostril, lip, or eyelid. This situation falls under the admonition to "horse-proof" your stall. Electrical tape wrapped enough times to fill the gap (even if you have to rewrap from time to time) should eliminate the hazard. Check that these are in place each time you refill buckets.

During the stall construction or preparation phase, make sure that all horizontal raw wood edges that are not butting up against other boards are covered with one-inch angle iron to prevent gnawing. Again, you need a drill, and this time, use self-tapping panhead screws to secure the metal. (These screws are round on top and do not present another sharp surface to worry about.) This is a step that you must not ignore, or you will regret it. A horse can chew through the top of a new board over the course of one night. The only exposed wood edges that will survive this onslaught are the ones that are vertical or above head high.

So without wood to chew, it is a good idea to provide some toys that are indestructible. Balls suspended from rafters along with a gravel-filled plastic milk jug and salt-on-a-rope securely fastened at head height all help to entertain the curious and bored ones.

Another stall element that needs to be completely secure is the stall door. Nothing is as reliable as a solid sliding wood door with a sliding bolt. Hinged double or half doors all eventually get pushed out or off their hinges. If a horse can see over the door, they will always try to push out through it. A yoked-style door is available but carries with it the same security issues and the added possibility for a horse to lunge over toward another horse or handler passing by. In addition, remember that any door that swings open takes up valuable aisle space when opening or closing. So your horse's need to see out can be met by leaving open a space at the back of sides of the stall that allows him to put his head out. If that is not possible, make it so. On the areas that require it, install a row of vertical metal bars (spaced six inches apart), especially over the trough and water buckets. (Feeding and watering are made so much easier without having to enter and leave the stall, and the bars allow for that.)

We installed a two-foot-trailer quick-escape tie on the outside of each stall at the feed trough. This allows me to secure each horse while they eat so that I can open the stall doors and work inside without them going out or getting in the way of the wheelbarrow and rakes. (This measure is not meant to be permanent, but it does work in the beginning when your horse needs to get accustomed to your routine.) It also provides a way to restrict the horse's access to water during cool-down periods.

Before leaving this chapter, let me address an issue that is permanent: the accumulation of dust everywhere in your stalls. Sawdust, hay, horse dander, and cobwebs make their way onto every surface and into every crevice. Regular hosing of walls and rafters and mats is a must. Keep the cobwebs under control, particularly in the fall. (They can be a fire hazard). Carefully eliminate dirt dauber and wasp nests that are visible. (These insects are anathema to horses. Most will not enter a stall, eat from a trough, or drink from a bucket if one of these insects is inside.) Hosing is the only way to carry out this dirty chore. According to our vet, one client had to have her horse treated for terrible chronic allergies. Everyone was at a loss to determine the cause until she revealed that she used a *leaf blower* to keep down the dust. Needless to say, she meant well and immediately stopped using that method. The horse recovered. Problem solved.

CHAPTER 4

The Barn Elements

*Whoever it is that leaves…(the
Morgan colt) out so late
When other creatures have gone to stall and bin,
Ought to be told to come and take him in…*

—From *The Runaway* by Robert Frost

The barn's footprint is compact—thirty-two feet wide and some thirty-five feet long. The structure includes sixty-year-old oak boards that were used as flooring from a dismantled tobacco warehouse in Danville, Virginia. The remaining materials are pressurized lumber. The aisle is L-shaped and a mere—five feet wide covered by seven—continuously laid end-to-end heavy stall mats on a gravel footing. The hay room is on the ground level, so pallets are used to keep the hay away from the floor. (This arrangement results in less dust raining down from overhead as in most barns.) The feed or tack room contains metal bins for feed (each holds 150 lbs. or 3 bags), and each lid is secured with a bungee cord across the lid. There is the extra convenience of a dorm-sized refrigerator that is necessary to keep medicines cool; in addition, there is a small can for loose salt and a storage bin for clean towels, braiding supplies, and clippers. Horseshoe hooks hold lead lines, halters, fly masks, crops, and small hand tools.

Two water hoses run through the barn area: one for both the inside area and one for the outside trough. They are both secured under the aisle mats for safety and protection in freezing temperatures. The inside length of hose has its own caddy to keep it clear from the aisle area. The wash stall and crossties are invaluable. Well lit, with bright LED bulbs, it is ideal for daily grooming, hoof cleaning, and clipping and braiding manes and tails. The farrier uses this area as well. The floor is concrete, poured with a slight slope to the outside wall of the barn. The water drains out immediately under the boards and eliminates the time-consuming chore of cleaning out a continuously clogged floor-mounted drain.

Wall-mounted square wire baskets eliminated the problem of water accumulation in them as well. We mounted them with the bottom against the wall, allowing access to the bottles from the front instead of up from the inside. This arrangement allows the separation of medicinal lotions and skin treatment products from shampoo and conditioners. The dual basket arrangement is used on the opposite wall, with two narrower ones separating grooming products from washing tools, hoof picks, and sweat scrapers.

The adjoining run-in shed has stall mats with a sawdust base also. The horses use this area in the heat of the day and as a buffer against the wind and rain. In addition to having salt available in their stalls, they have access to a solid mineral and salt blocks in feeders. These feeders are meant to be kept out of the weather, so this area serves that purpose.

A long metal gate on the end of the shed prohibits access to the riding ring. Conveniently, the shed area could be used as another stall if needed.

With regard to security, one added note that involves the aisle areas and sliding stall doors is the need to place a bump stop against the bottom of the doors on the opposite side of the latch. We use a short six-by-six piece of two feet long beam that when placed precisely creates a channel for the door to slide behind. (*Note: The wood should be short enough to serve as a doorstop but not long enough to be an obstacle that you and your horse will trip over when entering or leaving the stall.*) Also, the sliding stall doors hardware usually includes a bottom device that is a small wheel mounted on a metal rod that is driven into the floor flush with the door. These doorstop contraptions have had a very short life span at our barn. Our experience quickly pointed out the need for something much more durable and portable since you will have to move it to clean the door channel of sawdust.

The L-shaped aisle has two additional small gates: one oriented to the outside of the barn and the other inside to separate a loose horse from getting access to the other's stall. This inside gate also restricts access to the aisle in the area across from the wash stall.

The fan system in this small space has evolved overtime. We invested in four rail-mounted fan racks that tilt forward from overhead. One oversized fan blows over the wash stall from an outer wall and efficiently cools the first big stall. In short, the horses have a flow of direct air at both their grain feeders and hay areas. These fans run day and night from May to September. The blades can be carefully hosed off without affecting the integrity of the motor. It is best that they remain on to instantly blow out the spray. It is a fact that the longevity of the fans is based on the practice of always turning the power off by unplugging them or using the toggle switch on a power strip. *Never* try to turn off or adjust the switch on the fan. The connections in the switch tend to lock up from continued use and are best permanently left in the On-High position.

The maximum use of the fans provides additional benefits than the obvious; they dramatically reduce the need for fly spray applications in the stall, they help to dry out the bedding, and they help drown out startling noises from storms and holiday fireworks. Much attention has to be focused on the safe installation of any electrical device in your barn. Run heavy-duty drop cords overhead through rafters if possible. Check cords periodically for overheating; replace them immediately if any feel warm, or you detect the smell of anything you suspect is burning rubber. If it is necessary to have any short lengths of cord within reach of a horse, cut a matching length of old garden hose in half, pull the slit open, and encase the wire inside. Secure the hose to the wire with zip ties and then tighten the length of hose to the back of a board or post, making it as invisible and hard to reach as possible.

We have always been surprised at the problems other wildlife can cause at a horse barn. Opossums and raccoons, who are initially attracted by the availability of feed droppings, quickly develop a taste for the components that make up electrical wire. The resulting damage can match the destruction perpetrated by a horse and could pose another fire hazard.

Lack of order and organization pose other important safety issues. Consider always making a purposeful, attentive walk through the barn before you leave. The purpose for this action can be motivated by the possibility that the next time you enter the barn, your horses may meet you at the feed room door. In that event, you will want them to have done as little damage to themselves and your property as possible.

A barn safety checklist should include:

- *Recheck* the position of rakes, hoses, latches, gates, and the proper location of recently used equipment such as wheelbarrows, loose hay ropes, muck buckets, hay hooks, and tack. (*Note: There is an old superstition that says, "Putting away a dirty rake brings bad luck to a barn." My advice, ignore this at your own peril.*)
- *Assess* the status of each horse's water supply, grain ration, and hay needed for your feeding schedule.
- *Verify* the security of feed barrels, supplements, and medical supplies.
- *Add*, if needed, printed feeding directions in a visible, durable form.
- *Update* these directions immediately when any different situation arises.

None of us should be naive enough to think that we can eliminate every possible dangerous contingency when it comes to our horses. However, the following preventable incident was so shocking and so sudden that it has left an indelible impression on my approach to barn management. At an Arabian show in Lexington, Virginia, someone left a rake in an occupied stall. The horse was found with the end of the handle wedged in his nostril, and the brutality of his injury revealed that the force of the accident had caused it to penetrate his brain. *Double-check your equipment.*

My advice is to keep your horse up in the barn at night. My feeling is that we do so much to provide a safe environment for them in the daytime that leaving them out and to their own defenses at night is just not acceptable. In fact, for me, nothing I know is more comforting than knowing my horses are in a secure, comfortably, fresh-bedded stall at night with an ample supply of hay, no matter the severity of the weather.

CHAPTER 5

Water

You can lead a horse to water…and it turns out you can make him drink.

—H. B.

Metabolically, water is extremely important to the equine digestive system. They require five to ten gallons of fresh water daily. With one hundred feet of a complex gut system, the horse is at great risk from impaction colic without adequate water intake. (With this critical need in mind, add about half cup of loose salt to the feed trough about twice a week to encourage extra water consumption.)

My watering regimen is consistent—fresh buckets twice a day, with no exceptions. This never involves just topping off a low bucket. Standing water gets too warm and goes stale quickly in every stall environment. If the water is not fresh, that will never be the only option for my horses. It is suggested that you keep Clorox on hand and that you clean all buckets with a brush periodically. Be sure to follow up with a thorough rinse as most horses are very sensitive to the smell of their water. This results in their refusing to drink at all. This characteristic is made very apparent when the unprepared horseman loads up for a show weekend and realizes, on arrival, that his horses refuse to drink the local water. The solution is to acclimate the horse at home by slightly flavoring his water with spearmint drops or apple juice and then replicating that process away from home. Gatorade has been shown to be an effective additive and has the added benefit of electrolytes needed in hot weather.

The horse does ingest water (fluids) from grasses, particularly in spring and summer. You should simulate this process by shaking out flakes of hay when serving it and then thoroughly wetting down the piles. This simple method helps to prevent coughing and dust inhalation as well. Timing is important because most horses choose to drink water after finishing their grain ration, so make sure their buckets are filled beforehand. You will probably encounter several horses that will dip hay into the water buckets on their own. Save them this step and wet down the hay for all the horses in your barn.

Dehydration is a dangerous scenario in working and endurance horses. There are visible signs of this condition. It is routinely detected by horsemen using the skin "pinch" test. If the skin on the neck stays in the "pinched-up" position for five to ten seconds, immediate veterinary care should be administered.

Another consideration relates to the horses' winter water needs. This topic has generated much thought and ongoing experimentation. Some owners probably consider that they have met their horses' cold-weather-water needs by breaking the ice in their buckets and troughs. It turns out that if you want your horse to drink an adequate amount of water in winter, you should provide warm water (in the form created by a buckets and troughs with heater coils) as the only water source options. To clarify, Dr. Michaela Kristula, DVM of the New Bolton Center, reached this conclusion and elaborated by suggesting that if both warm bucket or trough sources and natural icy (stream water) are accessible, the horse will choose the extremely cold water. The concern arises when it was determined that the horses freely choosing the icy water will not ingest the preferred amount compared to that consumed by those with only tepid water options. In defense of the horse, the rationale for the high percentage of them choosing the colder water is that the horse has evolved to naturally equate cold water with fresh water, which, normally, would be the safest option for them.

Outside, the horses have a sixty-gallon water trough. These are best located in the shade, especially in summer, to keep the water cool. Cool water temperatures, combined with minimal sunlight, retards the growth of algae. While you can control algae, you cannot completely eliminate it, especially during the weeks when the temperatures and humidity combine to make summers unbearable. There are numerous additives and "fixes" circulating that do not lessen the algae problem and could compromise your horse's health. The tank will need cleaning with Clorox every four to five days. If it begins to look and smell like a fish tank, you have ignored the situation way too long. Certain type of algae can be extremely dangerous to horses, and there have been many recent reports of animal fatalities resulting, not only from ingestion, but casual contact.

Another deadly water habitat to be aware of is Potomac horse fever (PHF). Originally found in the 1980s, near Washington, DC, documented cases have spread to include forty-plus states and Canada. Freshwater snails and slugs deposit the affecting trematode (or fluke) into wetlands areas where it is ingested by caddis flies and the more common mayfly. It is believed that horses contract the disease through grazing these wet areas and ingesting the infected flies. The affected horse will exhibit a high fever and usually more debilitating symptoms, such as abortion in pregnant mares, along with colic, laminitis, founder, and death. Though still under study, this disease does not yet appear to pass from horse to horse.

A vaccine for PHF does exist—administered twice a year, in early spring and early summer, coinciding with the first emergence of the mayfly and then to provide a booster. The vaccines are not 100 percent effective in disease prevention but are shown to dramatically lessen the effects of exposure. Be proactive and discuss the risk of disease outbreaks in your immediate area with your veterinarian.

If vaccines are not available, you might mitigate the risk of a disease breakout by planting a riparian buffer around wetland areas on your property to discourage any emerging insects from migrating to your pasture areas.

Speaking in general conservation terms, another finding in the American Southwest has taken an animal rights cause in the first positive direction in years. After much discussion about the need to remove America's wild horse and burro populations (and the furor that engendered), it can now be documented that the members of these herds have developed a life-saving technique that went unexplained for decades. These horses and little burros are digging holes some six feet or more below the semi-arid surface to create their own water sources. These wells then affect the entire ecosystem of these areas by benefiting countless other forms of wildlife. Since discovered, we can hope that this behavior might just have a more long-term effect on their ability to exist in their natural habitat. Clearly, this is another example of the equine's extraordinary history of environmental adaptation. The list of the equine's contributions to the history of mankind continues to lengthen.

CHAPTER 6

Feeding the Complex Equine Digestive System

*Many have sighed for the good old days
and regretted the passing of the horse—
But today when only those who love them
own them, it is a far better time for horses.*

—C.W. Anderson

The stomach of the horse and the small intestine have the same function as those of dogs and cats, which are considered to be monogastric animals. The main difference in the complexity of the horse's digestive system is found in the large intestine, or hindgut, that can process the cellulose found in grass and vegetation. This hindgut includes a caecum and a colon. The caecum is the organ referred to earlier whose function depends on an adequate supply of water. The caecum is a fermentation container that breaks down the forage eaten by the horse. This is why horses can digest the same foods that ruminants eat. Know that unlike ruminants, a horse chews food completely the first time and swallows it. Their chewing movement is a lengthy, rhythmic, side-to-side motion similar to a ruminant. This extensive chewing helps to prepare the food for the fermentation process carried out in the upper part of the large intestine. It is the similarities of diet and chewing action that contribute to the incorrect assumption that horses have multiple stomach compartments. Adding to the confusion is the literal translation of Merychippus—Greek for "ruminant horse"—that referred to a prehistoric horse that resembled modern horses. The Greek name referred originally to the simple fact that this equine survived on grasses through grazing, not its stomach structure.

(*Note: Early scientists made erroneous assumptions about cows as well. Many of us have probably been told that the cow has four stomachs. That species of ruminant has four compartments to its stomach. Furthermore, the hippopotamus has three compartments, but it is not a ruminant. None of this was completely understood until veterinary hospitals such as NC State University installed a "window" or protected open wound called a "cannula" in a cow's body to see and analyze the contents of the stomach in its different compartments.*)

For the more practical purposes of feeding your horse, it is important to know that the capacity of a horse's stomach is a mere eight quarts. The stomach, ideally, is never more than two-thirds full due to the ingested food moving out of the stomach within thirty to forty-five minutes on average. It takes thirty-six to seventy-two hours for a bite of food to form as manure. Elimination then occurs four to thirteen times per day. Horses produce a large amount of saliva (some ten gallons) while eating. The volume of saliva neutralizes stomach acids that could otherwise cause gastric ulcers. Therefore, horses benefit from having a constant supply of free choice, preferably cool-season grass hay like orchard grass. (Cool season grasses grow during "cool" spring and fall months and are baled soon after.) Orchard grass has an acceptable level of 8 to 13 percent crude protein and a calcium content of 0.26 to 0.27 percent. My hay is a locally preferred combination of Orchard grass and Fescue (which is another type of cool grass that grows well in our heavy clay soil. This hay combination is ideal for those of us with less available grass and needs to increase our amount of forage for horses that have IR. This exact hay combination revealed a 7 percent sugar level that falls well within the range of acceptability for horses with this condition.

None of these figures would matter if the horse will not eat the hay you provide. It helps that these bales have great color, a sweet aroma, and small palatable stems. To my great satisfaction, my horses always clean up their entire ration. Their nutritional needs depend on their forage since their grain servings are necessarily less than average.

As stated earlier, all horses benefit when their hay flakes have been shaken out, separated, and thoroughly hosed down. Even the best hay supplier cannot always control the occasional briers, leaves, hay rope fragments, or other undesirable things that get into the baler. Shaking out the hay allows you to remove those things before they become part of your horse's meal or his bedding. Most horse owners feed hay on the stall floor or on the ground outside. This method has the advantage of encouraging proper drainage of your horse's extensive sinus cavity system. My two horses share one-half of a bale of hay outside during their pasture turn-out time during the day. They alternate between grazing and eating hay which, again, indicates the importance of buying quality forage. So the remaining half bale is divided for the evening feeding inside the barn. The amount of hay fed should be consistent and well thought out. (If your horse does not clean up his hay, you are either feeding too much, or something is "off" with the hay.)

The rule about gradually introducing new feed is based on another complex process in the horses' digestive process. Sudden changes in diet result in microbes and bacteria that cannot "keep up" in the needed fermentation process.

In the intricate process of digestion, colic often occurs when there is not enough water intake for food to enter and exit the caecum. This structure is known as the "blind gut," precisely because of this movement in and out of the same orifice at the top of the caecum. This condition is referred to as caecal impaction, which is a very specific origin of pain. (Colic is a general term for abdominal pain in the horse without identifying the cause or location.)

The intent of this discussion is to focus on those feeding conditions over which horse owners have some control through our choices of food and the amounts of water we provide.

In addition, there is a proactive approach that can be employed to stay ahead of digestive problems. Be aware of your horses' normal "gut sounds." You can easily monitor those noises by listening to your horse by placing your ear to the belly. Noises indicate that food is moving. If your horse is displaying some worrisome behaviors—including refusing food, restlessness, sweating, or trying to lay down—check the gut sounds. If no noises are present, your horse needs immediate veterinary intervention.

While every feeding regimen is different, the following reflects the regimen we have adopted to balance our available turn-out space, grass availability, and the individual health needs of our horses. My grain ration consists of a pelleted, 12 percent protein, low carbohydrate feed. Distributed by Southern States Cooperative, this feed is sold under the brand name Nutrena. Their Select Plus Pellets are free of dust and easy to feed even in cold weather. The horses are fed twice a day—half of a standard three-quart flat bottom scoop. This is the amount recommended by my vet based on concerns she has about both horses having similar physical characteristics from the same sire. (They both display the thick crest, which is found in many horses that eventually develop Cushings and insulin resistance.) My mare and gelding are both seven years old and are "easy keepers." However, it is a delicate process to find a method to maintain an ideal weight for any horse—particularly, those who get light exercise and depend on busy horse owners to find the right balance for them. It is worth the effort, however, because being overfed and overweight has very serious long-term consequences for your horse.

One of the violent and deadly outcomes for the overfed horse is a rupture of the stomach. Many of us have long been aware of the horse's inability to vomit. Once considered a unique trait in the horse, we now know that other mammals (rodents in particular) have a "one-way" digestive system (which, anecdotally, is why rat poison is so effective in that population.) The horse's limitation is due to the location of a band of muscle that surrounds the esophagus where it enters the stomach. This acts as a restricting, cut-off valve muscle. If a horse does vomit, it is due to a ruptured stomach from grain overconsumption, ingestion of indigestible feeds, or taking in large quantities of cold water. All of which causes a fatal gastric distention and the consequential rupture.)

The most startling reaction to a feeding issue that I have ever witnessed occurred in our pony. Dixie was a typical pasture pet that we would occasionally hand graze in our yard. Imagine the shock of seeing her walking toward me with a garden-hose volume of saliva pouring from her mouth. She was clearly in distress, and the saliva continued to stream. Hypersalivation can be caused by a clover fungus, or a toxic mushroom. (It may seem inaccurate to see the volume of saliva produced by the horse to be nearly ten gallon until you actually see such a reaction.) Thankfully, the vet was able to administer an antidote that "switched off" the reaction within minutes. Otherwise, IV fluids would have been needed and the prognosis would have been in doubt. (Horses do not typically eat mushrooms, but fungus-infected clover presents a more common threat.)

One major advantage that today's horse owners take comfort in is the wide assortment of available feed supplements available today. Consult with your veterinarian before starting a regimen because of the complicating factors that might result. Concerning drug and food interactions in horses are not unlike those in humans.

InsulinWise is a powdered veterinary formula that my horses receive at each of the two daily feedings. It is for horses with IR. The recommended dose is half scoop (measured in a one-ounce scoop included in the container). It is mixed with about two tablespoons of unsweetened applesauce and stirred in with their grain pellets. The scientific studies on InsulinWise have shown that the product is very effective in horses with IR and can be safely used in those with a genetic predisposition to develop the condition. Thankfully, this product is safe to use indefinitely.

With IR and weight control in mind, we have to also think of the impact of the treats we feed. If you reevaluate their importance, they actually fall into the supplement category. The following traditional treats, such as apples, pears, and cherries have been eliminated from my choices. They not only have a high sugar content but are the source of a hidden danger. The seeds of these fruits contain cyanide. When metabolized in the digestive system, the toxin degrades into hydrogen cyanide. (Those fairy tales featuring "poison apples" were way ahead of our modern science.)

Fortunately, blueberries (the "super food" with antioxidants) are also a safe, convenient treat that horses love. Remember that these are food supplements, so do not overfeed any treats. Also, blueberries and other fruits should be rinsed before feeding. This allows you to discard any berries that show signs of rot or mold.

In closing, if as a horse owner you have found yourself referring to "fat" as your favorite color of horse, you may want to reevaluate that emotional response to overfeeding and frequent treats. We would all do well to remember that we have taken part in dramatically changing the domestic horse's environment—less exercise, more stall time, and processed food fed in overly large meals. We have changed the environment to suit our needs. However, the horse, as evolved as he is, cannot adapt to these changes and thrive unless his owner adjusts his needs to meet those of his horse.

CHAPTER 7

Grooming and Skin Care

Horses may be more sensitive to pain than originally thought originally referred to as thick-skinned, the horse's skin is thicker than human skin by only 1 millimeter.

—Dr. Lydia Tong, Australian Veterinary Pathologist

The continued complexity of the horse's anatomy is evident in the structure and function of its largest organ—the skin. Keratin gives it a water-resistant property and aids in preventing internal evaporation. Parasites are met with a highly acidic pH and can enter the body through breaks in the skin. Extensive nerve endings are responsible for a horse being able to feel the slightest pressure from the landing of a fly. Besides the obvious ability to cool off through body sweat, the horse also has sweat glands in the frog of the hoof.

The horse has three distinct types of hair: the permanent hair that makes up the mane and tail; tactile hairs that are on the muzzle and around the eyes; and the regular coat that grows and sheds based on exposure to natural seasonal light.

The benefits of daily grooming become more apparent in light of the horse's need to maintain skin health. This ritual is a comforting interaction between horse and owner that is best established long before formal training and riding begins. This close contact is a way to check for health issues and to increase blood flow to the surface of the skin. Only a slight accumulation of dirt, combined with moisture, causes irritation to the horse's oversensitive skin.

The best grooming schedule should include brushing twice a day (during feeding). Hooves should be picked out after every turn-out session. My horses show a preference for soft, dandy brush because it can be used on the legs and the face. Curry combs (no metal, only rubber) are for unusual accumulations of mud. The metal curry combs should be used to clean the hair and debris from your body brushes. Never neglect the underbelly of your horse. It is a sensitive area and most of the wet mud or sand accumulations will be under that area. If you are preparing to ride, carefully groom the girth area and the saddle area of the horse's back.

Brush in the direction of the hair growth in sensitive bony areas. Use a circular motion with slight pressure when using the curry comb. Dip the body brush in water (preferably collected rainwater) to brush through manes and tails that either need "training," or that need added stimulation to grow out.

Be aware that the other underbelly areas that need cleaning are the sheath and the udder. The sheath of a gelding develops a layer of smegma—a thick, oily or sticky lubricating material, that when combined with dirt and bedding material residue can build up to form "beans" that can cause swelling and restrict urination. It is recommended that cleaning take place only every six to twelve months. Excalibur makes an excellent product that can be applied to soften and remove this material gently. It is necessary to rinse this area well with as much water as the horse will tolerate. The udder of the mare accumulates material as well and needs more frequent cleaning. Excalibur can be used for washing the whole udder area, but particularly between the teats. Again, be very careful to rinse well and dry the area gently. A small amount of Vaseline petroleum jelly can be applied to soothe any irritation and as a barrier to further accumulation of matter until the next cleaning.

Another mixture that does double duty at the barn is WD-40 lubricant and baby oil. Combine these in a spray bottle (five parts WD-40 to one part baby oil) to use as a mane or tail detangler. You will want to use this method year-round, but it also helps to eliminate dryness in the winter when washing and conditioning is not a convenient option. It is safe to reapply a small spray to the mane after daily hosing off in the summer. Use freely on a freshly washed tail and in between washings when you are grooming the tail unless your horse's tail is braided.

Full flowing long tails are a desirable trait in many horse breeds. Unlike the practical "banged tails" of hunters and jumpers, the tails of many breeds, including those of Tennessee walking horses, are maintained to be as long as possible—sometimes trailing on the ground behind them. (Hair extensions are often used to achieve this effect if needed.) My two horses have incredibly long tails, so braiding is the only way to be confident that they can be turned out without risking the damage that might occur without supervision. Flat-shod Walking Horses show without a tail set. So the following braiding technique works for a natural tail and does not require any daily maintenance:

Before braiding, wash and let tail dry. "Pick out" the tail strand by strand. Spray liberally with WD-40 mixture and comb through.

1. Start a three-strand braid *below* the root of the tail. Braid down the length, stopping about eight inches above the end.
2. Using electrical tape, wrap the end of the braid with the tape moving up the tail for about five inches and back down to secure the tape *on* the tape. (You now have a braided tail with a loose brush of hair at the bottom for fly flicking.) What makes this worth the time and effort is how you tie up the braid from this step.
3. Bend the braided end of the tail toward the horse and thread it through one of the loops and pull it out of the braid to the front—bend front. Bend the taped part down and hold the now three-braided sections on top of each other.
4. Start wrapping the tape around the three sections (leaving the brush of hair still hanging free). Wrap the entire triple

section until secure (make sure the tail section is able to hang down straight) and cut the end of the tape from the roll and secure the end.

At this point, it is critical to make sure that there is no pressure being applied to the root of the tailbone. Feel down through the braid to find the tailbone. Never put any tape in this area, even though stray hairs will work their way out of the top of the braid, which is one reason you will probably want to redo this after two or three weeks. In winter, you can do the same procedure without washing—merely picking out and brushing out the oil residue (which will be black and oily) before reapplying it and re-braiding.

The benefit of this braid is that you can see what the condition of the tail is at any time, which would not be possible if you use a tail bag or other wraps. Also, it will dry naturally if the horse gets wet, and it will not easily get hung on anything.

One last point about the tail: check the appearance of the end of the tailbone when washing. If your horse is rubbing his tail, there could be some irritation present that you would not be aware of otherwise. Medicated shampoos are readily available for those issues.

As many styles of manes and tails exist as there are breeds of horses. At least one misconception about achieving these looks has been cleared up with more scientific research. The old method of "mane pulling" to shorten and thin the manes of thoroughbreds for braiding does cause discomfort to the horse. This procedure was once believed to be acceptable because it was thought that the horse did not feel the hair pulling. Instead, we now know that there are nerve endings in the hair follicles of the mane and tail. The misconception that horses do not have feeling in the mane and tail comes from most of them simply tolerating the procedures we inflict on them. Now, most use a more humane way to achieve the "pulled mane" effect that involves teasing the short hair back in a small section and razoring off the long pieces. In general, it is best not to ever cut a horse's mane with scissors. It takes a long time for the mane to grow out, and it will have a more natural look if you take the time to thin it correctly.

Clipping is an important element of the grooming process, and the following are the areas that should be kept trimmed to give your horse a professionally groomed look:

- *Muzzle and eye areas.* Long whiskers can get caught and be rubbed when bridling. Trim the tactile hairs from both areas (the long eye hairs above and below the eye can grow in toward the eye and cause irritation).
- *Throatlatch.* Keep the area under the jawline neatly trimmed for a more refined look the head poll. Trim a bridle path on mane at the top of the neck between the ears and down the mane in a length determined by your breed preferences. Also, trim a strip of hair (the width of the clipper blade) on each side of the trimmed mane.
- *Forelock.* Trim a small area underneath the forelock on the face to allow the hair to lay flat on the face and a small length on the left side to allow the foretop to be tucked neatly pulled to the right under the browband of the bridle.
- *Feet.* Clip the long hairs that grow down over the coronet band around the hoof (this looks best if you trim in an upward motion). Clip the back of the fetlock (be careful of the bony cartilage areas).
- *Ears.* It is best not to clip the hair away from the inside of your horse's ears. I trim only the outside edges and the tufts of hair that grow out from the bottom. (If you are showing, you would want to clip the inside and keep the clipped ear moist with a bit of baby oil to deter gnats in the summer.)

(*Note: Clippers will have to be replaced every couple of years. Wahl Cordless Clippers have the best run time and needless maintenance if you keep them away from temperature extremes and humidity.*)

My horses like grooming, but they love being washed. There are many shampoos and conditioners for horses. The drugstore brand of TRESemmé shampoo and conditioner are cost-efficient, mild, and rinse out easily. After the first full spring bath, I usually wash with conditioner only. Never use either product on the horse's face. Mist the face gently, giving the horse time to adjust his eyes and ears to the spray. Extremely careful to avoid the ears. Daily hosing off is essential in summer. It is also a good idea to wash off the fly spray for stall time and reapply the next day.

The old-style hand-lever hose nozzle allows you to quickly control the pressure of the water with one hand. Start with the back legs, particularly if the horse has just been worked and is very hot (too much cold weather on the chest area causes stress on the heart of a hot horse).

Use a sweat scraper; the curved, rubber-edged type is better tolerated than the straight metal kind. Use small towels to wipe the horse down. Start with the face, particularly under the chin, the nostrils. Wipe over the eyes and around the ears. Dry the lower legs, down the fetlocks and underbelly particularly. (Remember, horses love for you to rub the areas for them that they cannot reach. This is another part of the bonding process.)

The wash stall is the best place to clean out your horse's feet and to apply hoof dressing. When working with a horse that is not always willing to cooperate with this phase of grooming, set yourself up for success. In the rear, shift your horse's weight from the hoof you need to pick up. The one he has his weight on is the hoof that is farther to the rear. He is not going to give you that foot, so move him over and readjust his weight. My gelding has to be sedated every time my farriers work on him; but, strangely, he will allow me to hose his feet out in the wash stall by using this weight-shifting method. (By the way, the position of the front feet has little effect on this issue.)

CHAPTER 8

Skin Diseases

*A good man will take care of his horses,
not only while they are young, but also
when they are old and past service.*

—Plutarch

The following is a list of the most common equine skin conditions. The severity of each can be mitigated through early detection during regular grooming.

(*Note: This list is solely intended to share skin issues that I have seen manifested in horses and have worked through with the advice of a veterinarian. This discussion is meant to help the novice determine how skin abnormalities may appear in order to accurately describe your horse's condition to your veterinarian.*)

- *Rain rot or rain scald.* This condition is one of the few that is not as serious as it looks. This issue is very common and is caused by bacteria that flourish in warm wet conditions. It can also develop on the topline in winter when the horse is blanketed and sweats during temperature fluctuations. It might first appear as crusty, scaly areas on the back and rump, basically mimicking the pattern that rainwater makes as it runs off the horse's back. The hair sticks together to form slender tufts that can easily be pulled or brushed out. Medicated shampoos and sprays used daily are very effective. (Banixx and Banixx Spray are recommended.)

- *Ringworm*. This fungus initially looks like a simple patchy hair loss. There is no inflammation or skin trauma from rubbing. It is best to clip around the area, leaving a clear margin that will allow you to spot-treat the lesions. Betadine scrub, rinsed with a white vinegar or water solution, is an effective treatment that creates an acidic environment that deters the spread of the ringworm fungi. While this situation usually resolves in about fourteen days, it is spread quite easily to house pets as well as humans. Take care to disinfect clippers and clothing during the treatment phase. The horse experiencing this ailment benefits from dry outside weather conditions and the healing effects of the sun's ultraviolet light.

- *Scratches (mud fever or dew poisoning)*. Visually, this is one of the worst horse ailments. To the horse, it is certainly one of the most painful to endure. Thankfully, it is also one of the easiest to prevent. It occurs on the pasterns and fetlocks of horses that are exposed to constant mud and moisture. Visually, this condition begins as pink ulcerations that turn into thick crusty scabs that cause swelling. These areas need to be clipped without disturbing the scabs. Use Banixx Shampoo with mild ingredients that do not sting to kill the fungus. This disease can be easily transferred from horse to horse, so take extreme care with your towels and supplies. Scratches is more common in horses with white socks and legs because the unpigmented skin is more easily irritated. Also, draft horses are more susceptible due to the heavy feathering of their lower legs. The feathering traps moisture, and a problem can develop before it can be easily seen. Mud is not the only concern with this issue. As its other name implies, it is best to avoid early morning turnout when there is heavy cold dew on high grass.

- *Summer sore.* This is both a complicated and a devastatingly injurious condition in horses that is very specific despite its seemingly generic name. The file pictures of these wounds are very difficult for horse owners to view. It is a rare condition these days, but there has been a resurgence of cases in the last three or four years. According to D. G. Pugh, DVM of Auburn University College of Veterinary Medicine, the incidences of summer sore were drastically reduced with the development of ivermectin as a horse wormer. This disease is characterized by a sore that will not heal, but it is how the sore develops that makes it complicated. The worm larvae from common stomach worms in horses find their way back into the body through an external wound, sheath, or membranes of the vulva. The same larvae do far less damage to the horse in their natural stomach environment but externally create wounds that will not heal on their own. Diligent veterinary care, manure management, and a systematic worming program helps to prevent this terrible situation.
- *Sweet itch.* According to Deidre Carson and Sidney Ricketts, sweet itch is a true hypersensitivity to saliva from biting insects or midges. The affected horse will experience intense itching and rub himself raw on anything that is available—sometimes rubbing out a mane or tail dock completely. This reaction is believed to be a genetic predisposition that can emerge in a young horse and, unfortunately, increase in severity each summer season as they age. Topical treatments merely relieve the itching but do not cure the condition. If possible, the horse should be moved to areas without standing or flowing water which harbor the larvae of the biting insects. Hoods and sheets can also be used to reduce the area exposed to biting. The insects in question are the most active between the hours of 4:00 p.m. and 7:00 a.m., so it is advised to keep your horse stabled during these times.

- *Warts.* Papilloma virus (a horse-specific virus) is the cause of warts in horses. It is not a form that is transferable to humans but can be spread to other horses. They appear as raised pinkish-gray cauliflower structures that are usually located on the muzzle or lips. These usually shrink and disappear on their own. Surgical procedures may be employed for the cosmetic benefits needed for show horses. If the ear syndrome develops, it will cause white plaques inside the ears, which are permanent. Conley-Koontz Equine Hospital warns that this ear condition causes a sensitivity that makes it difficult for a handler to touch or work around the ears. Further, they suggest that fly masks with ear covers will make the horse less susceptible to insects that are attracted to the ear plaques.

(Note: This list of common skin diseases is not meant to be inclusive. The diseases are common in the sense that I have seen horses and owners struggle with the effects of each and the challenges of treating these overtime. They also have a similar pattern over a short period of time. Skin trauma becomes a sore, a sore becomes a wound, and a wound becomes a full-blown infection with swelling and pain in the average horse's environment. [It is also wise to consider that general immunodeficiency could be the root cause of skin conditions that persist or recur].)

CHAPTER 9

Characteristics of the Hoof

The horse moved like a dancer, which is not surprising. A horse is a beautiful animal, but he is perhaps most remarkable because he moves as if he always hears music.

—A Winter's Tale

The horse is classified as an ungulate or hoofed mammal. The hoof is essentially a large toe that evolved as a feature to benefit the horse in its natural grassland habitat. The hoof is an extension of the horse's long legs that are necessary to increase its running speed. The hoofed mammals are classified as cloven-hooved or odd-toed in the case of the horse.

The hoof would appear to be a fairly simple structure as anatomy texts refer to it being made up of only three main parts: the wall, the sole, and the frog. Though these areas are indeed clearly delineated, the hoof is anything but simple. The wall is the part of the hoof that is visible when the horse is standing—made up of the toe quarters and heel. The wall is a tough horn-like material that must be trimmed off due to continuous production. There are no nerves or blood vessels in the hoof wall.

The underside of the hoof reveals the V-shaped frog, sole, and bars of the wall. The normal sole does not contact the ground;

the frog touches the ground first in the motion of the horse. The three structures of the wall, bars, and frog are considered to be the weight-bearing structures.

The University of Missouri team of Robert C. McClure, Gerald R. Kirk, and Phillip D. Garrett have written extensively on the subject of the complexities of the inner structure of the hoof. They explain that the inside of the hoof contains several structures that change shape with compression (weight-bearing) and act as a pump to push the blood up into the leg. They further describe these areas as the digital cushion and highlight the critical need for exercise to increase circulation and to contribute to good hoof growth.

Anyone familiar with the training of horses is constantly aware of the instinctive "flight-or-fight" response. One can imagine how many undomesticated horses were unable to survive when "flight" was not an option due to lameness. *Gravel* and *laminitis* are the two most incapacitating types of lameness that the horse can encounter. Fortunately, the writings of Denise Steffanus for the *Paulick Report* have made the gravel issue less complicated for the horse owner. She explains that the "gravel" can be one of many types of fine particles that lodge in the white line area of the underside of the horse's hoof (usually in an unshod horse.) A particle can also enter through a nail hole, crack, or weak hoof wall. Infection builds and intense, sudden pain ensues, leaving the horse unable to put any weight on the affected hoof. Because of the "pumping" mechanism, the infection slowly works its way up to the surface and bursts through to exit the coronet band, causing the pressure to be immediately released. (The worst case is a subsolar abscess in which the infection goes underneath the sole, which causes even more distress and pain for the horse because there is not any way for the horse to place weight on any part of the hoof without extreme pain.) The conscientious horse owner needs to know how to resolve this condition as quickly as possible and to be aware of the environmental factors that make this such a common issue. Soft feet (from wet surfaces, including daily bathing or hosing) make the hoof more vulnerable. Your farrier should be called immediately to pressure "test" the sole to locate the abscess; he can pare away the sole to relieve the buildup of infection and start the drainage process. Next, the area needs to be soaked with an antibiotic spray and wrapped for up to forty-eight hours. Epsom salt poultices come in a variety of combinations and are beneficial in the healing process. The area should then be allowed to dry out to facilitate healing. Your veterinarian should administer a tetanus shot if needed as soon as the gravel diagnosis has been made.

Steve Norman, a farrier in the thoroughbred industry, cautions the zealous horse owner that one of the contributing factors in weakening a horse's hoof could be the overuse of hoof preparations. The inside of the hoof wall is made up of many straw-like tubes that can conduct the preparation material into the hoof from a leak into a nail hole and make the horse more susceptible to a gravel emergency.

Another hoof condition that your farrier may detect is *seedy toe*. This situation can result as a consequence of chronic laminitis or a long toe-low heal combination. Also referred to as *white line disease*, this takes the form of a bacterial infection that weakens the keratin, resulting in the telltale flaking off or rumbling of the hoof. The initial treatment includes trimming away as much of the infected area of the hoof as possible. The veterinarian will recommend a liquid cleaning antimicrobial agent. The follow-up treatment should include an established regular trimming regimen and possible shoeing to reestablish soundness. You are advised to keep stalls clean and dry and clean hooves daily to prevent reoccurrence.

Thrush is one hoof disease that you can easily detect yourself when you are cleaning your horse's feet. It is an infection characterized by a particularly foul-smelling discharge at the center or on the sides of the frog. The infection may be either bacterial or fungal. Horses with long heels develop deep, narrow frogs that are more prone to develop thrush. If left unattended, the infection may impact the deeper tissues of the hoof and cause swelling in the lower leg. Treatment involves the administration of a tetanus vaccine and the removal of the affected frog material. The sole of the foot should be scrubbed with a dilute iodine solution, and the horse should be housed in a clean dry stall. You might expect complete recovery from thrush within fourteen days.

(*Note: Tetanus has been mentioned repeatedly as a factor in recovery for several conditions. It should be clear that this vaccination should be kept updated in your attempt to minimize the effects of hoof infections.*)

Kopertox by Zoetis Inc. is a very effective preparation that can be applied daily at the first sign of thrush. The product should be applied according to its specific directions so as to avoid irritation to the horse's skin.

Of all the hoof ailments your horse is subject to, *laminitis* is the clearest threat to him being able to function normally after treatment. It is expensive to treat, extraordinarily time-consuming, and the owner goes through each debilitating phase not sure of the outcome. Multiple tests are needed to assess the initial damage done to the hoof and more to establish the permanent damage.

The coffin bone inside the hoof is the target of the laminitis condition. A radiograph shows the distinctive hoof-shaped bone inside the hoof. In a normal foot, in a side view, the front sloping angle of the coffin bone should be parallel to the outside angle of the hoof wall. With laminitis, the coffin bone rotates (or sinks down) with the tip of the bone pointing more directly down toward the inside sole. (It is this movement of the bone that causes such extreme sudden pain and lameness in the horse's front feet.) Laminitis can occur in the rear hooves, but it is more easily identified in the front weight-bearing legs. Radiograph imagery is used to determine the extent of the rotation. As the horse slowly regains normal movement and weight-bearing, the veterinarian knows that the rotation has ceased and will schedule another radiograph to ascertain the lasting permanent damage (or final position of the angle of the coffin bone). These readings are used by the farrier to gradually trim and angle the hoof to match the repositioning of the coffin bone. The heel is lowered to shift weight from the toe to the heel. Usually, the veterinarian recommends that a shoe one size larger be used to realign the weight and, thereby, make the horse more comfortable in his recovery. It is advised to have the farrier scheduled at six weeks intervals to gradually trim down the heels. Remember that the coffin bone and the hoof wall are virtually parallel in the normal hoof; that is, what you and your team are trying to reestablish in your horse.

(*Note: The coffin bone's position will not ever realign. The horse owner must make every effort to prevent recurrence because the diagnosis of founder [the critical last phase of laminitis] and its repercussions loom closer and more dire with each laminitis bout.*)

Amy Young of the UC Davis Center for Equine Health states that the clinical description of laminitis is damage to the hoof and tissue near the coffin bone. She explains that severe cases of laminitis lead to *founder* in which the coffin bone rotates to completely separate from the hoof.

No comfort should be taken in the knowledge that most veterinarians consider ponies and older horses to be more susceptible to laminitis. The fact is, there are many causes that affect all horses of any age:

- Excessive grain.
- High sugar levels in pasture.
- Injury in one foot that causes the horse to shift his weight to the other for a prolonged period.
- Ingestion of toxic plants.
- Excessive work on hard surface.

In addition, there are two equine diseases that can lead to or compound laminitis:

- Equine metabolic syndrome (EMS).
- Cushings' disease (pituitary pars intermedia dysfunction [PPID]).

Extreme lameness is the first visible sign of laminitis—usually in the front legs. The affected horse will shift their weight to the rear and pivot by raising up to avoid pressure on the front legs. The horse must have access to a heavily bedded stall so they can stand as comfortably as possible. (There is always a danger when lame horses resort to laying down for long periods of time.)

According to my veterinarian, Dr. Natalie Barker, there are at least four ways that you can reduce your horse's risk for laminitis:

- Limit lush pasture grazing time (particularly in the spring).
- Minimize sugars and carbohydrates in grain.
- Schedule regular farrier care.
- Arrange for daily exercise.
- Control your horse's weight.

CHAPTER 10

Dollar's Crisis: Facing Mortality

This is the most difficult part to recall and write. I have never lost a horse to anything but old age. I did not lose one this time, but we came so close; it is very hard to relive. There is merit in the retelling, and my gelding Dollar deserves credit for the strength and patience he showed me in the struggle.

It was fall in the first year of COVID-19, and the only family member that was showing any respiratory problem symptoms was my six-year-old gelding. Big and strong with a personality to match, Dollar and his half-sister, Skye, had come to us two years before and helped me realize my retirement dream to start over with young horses. (I had lost my last Arabian gelding and ironically thought my young horses would be bulletproof and worry-free from age-related illnesses.) Dollar and Skye had been here long enough for me to care passionately about them and their well-being.

The care and attention that they receive is as structured and planned with attention to detail as the writing of this manuscript. After a stunning accident that involved the tearing of an eyelid and the suturing that followed, it did occur to me that Dollar might be accident prone, or at least the target of our barn cat's wrath. I did make a mental note to make sure these two would both need to have regular vaccines, just in case. Then Dollar started with a cough and some nasal discharge. I redoubled my efforts to minimize dust by increasing the time spent wetting down his hay and took comfort in the fact that his pelleted grain ration is basically dust free. He had no other symptoms and no sinus infection.

The cough persisted and cold weather was approaching. Dollar's favorite vet, Dr. Natalie Barker from Chatham Equine Hospital, detected a narrowing of his airway and prescribed a course of steroids. Over the next ten days, the cough lessened with his staggered doses of three, then two, then one tablet daily. The morning of the very last day of dosage, he was shockingly crippled by laminitis. Dr. Barker came immediately and told me, to the dismay of us all, that Dollar was one of a low percentage of horses whose laminitis can be triggered by steroids.

Dr. Barker's blood tests confirmed what she suspected, but Dollar's high (off the chart) readings indicated the need for quick impactful intervention. She prescribed metformin tablets to counteract the effects of equine metabolic syndrome that resulted in the severe laminitis that seemingly developed over night. The dosage of thirty pills per day (fifteen, twice daily) may seem excessive, but the first six hundred pills did decrease Dollar's high numbers. Dr. Barker did another blood test that showed that it would be best to go through another twenty days of metformin (another six hundred tablets) to get the numbers down to a normal range.

Daily walking—painful to us both—only a mere handful of grain to get the crushed pills down, and cold, icy soaked hay could not have been pleasant for this patient horse of mine. The hay-soaking issue was necessary to reduce the naturally occurring sugar in the hay. Soaked hay is an awful heavy mess to manage. Considering that hay was basically all Dollar could safely eat, I bought a large plastic storage container with wheels. (It would easily hold four full flakes of hay.) The hay tote was filled with enough water to cover the hay, which had to soak for at least an hour. The process is interesting when you realize the brown water that is left over indicates that you have achieved your purpose because it is the excess sugar in the hay that turns the water brown. The metformin, the reduced grain, and the low sugar content in the hay is the formula to get the horse's insulin regulated. (*Note: Veterinarians advise that oversoaking the hay robs the grass of almost all its nutritional value. So if you find yourself in this situation, do not try to cut corners by soaking all day or all night to save time.)*

By the time we began the second round of metformin, Dr. Barker had taken radiographs to accurately determine how much rotation Dollar was experiencing. His lameness dissipated after about eight days, so we were pleased to see that he had a mild less than four-degree change in angle. He tolerated his numerous pills and had no change in bowel movements or disposition. He stopped laying down due to pain, even though he was on phenylbutazone (bute) for only two days. These seemed to be all positive signs, and Dr. Barker continued to patiently reassure me.

Winter set in and created a hay-soaking nightmare. The water at the barn was frozen until midday and so we had to find a solution. We wrapped our plastic tote in electric heat tape, secured by electrical tape, to keep the water in the tote ice-free. Tractor Supply carries large infrared heat lamps, so we hung one securely over the top of the tote. The hay-soaking ritual took shape. Fill the tote with water at night. Go down an hour before feeding to add the hay to soak. Feed, dump the water, and repeat for the evening feeding. I had to use rubber gloves to handle the wet hay and have battery-operated heated gloves to warm up and continue the barn chores. The ordeal seemed endless, but Dollar was making such extraordinary progress that it was well worth it.

Our eight-week farrier visit fit in perfectly with the waning last doses of metformin. Dr. Barker adjusted her schedule to consult with Eddie and Craig Martin to agree on the results of the last radiograph so they could adjust Dollar's hoof angles accordingly. The Martin team followed the veterinarian's recommendations to the letter and moved our farrier visits up to six-week intervals to make sure they stayed ahead of any changes in Dollar's condition.

To follow up, Dr. Barker sent off a hay sample for analysis. Dollar's second blood work came back, indicating his numbers were close to normal. The sugar content of my hay turned out to be low enough that we were able to stop soaking (though I still wet it thoroughly every day for every feeding). Dollar is now on a lifetime regimen of InsulinWise to manage his predisposition to EMS. He gets a modest one-third scoop of low carb-pelleted feed twice a day to control his weight. He enjoys daily turnout to ensure he gets enough exercise. My goal is to follow Dr. Barker's recommendations for Dollar's well-being in every area. She gave me very clear guidelines for early spring grazing. All horses benefit from limited time on pasture when the grass is green and lush. The small amount of acreage that the horses have access to is once again a safer option. What we imposed was a very strict fifteen-minute limit in the mornings for a week, then increased to twenty minutes for the second week. Thirty minutes, forty-five, and an hour followed until the weather warmed significantly and the danger of the sugar levels lessened naturally.

As we approach the one-year mark, we continue to monitor Dollar's weight and overall health. He has developed a severe case of sweet itch this summer, which Dr. Barker attributes to his overall sensitivity. We continue to monitor his weight, and she has advised that we need to do another blood test this fall since all horses see a spike in their numbers as the season changes to cooler weather. I will be scheduling a test.

Thank you to Dr. Barker and Dr. Erwin who collaborated in the effort to bring this exceptional horse back to normal. I am so grateful to my new farrier team, Eddie and Craig Martin. You changed your travel schedule to accommodate us when we needed you. I know this could easily have had a more dire outcome without you all.

CHAPTER 11

Blankets and Halters: The Debate

Two horses were in a pasture—one without blankets and one with three blankets
Unblanketed horse—"Why do your owners put so many blankets on you?"
Blanketed horse—"Because they're cold!"

—J. L. Werner

Horse owners all have strong opinions about whether or not to leave halters on horses at pasture and whether or not to blanket in winter. When you consider that most young horses are playful and difficult to catch, halter wearing probably begins as a temporary measure to condition the horse to being handled and making it all a quiver, more convenient process for the owner. Overtime, having your horse wearing a halter can simply become a habit that you see no reason to change.

At the very least, take the time to make sure any halter you use is snug and well fitting, with the throat latch snap opening positioned to touch the horse's jaw. The fear, of course, is that a loose halter can get hung, or a hoof can get lodged, particularly in the case of a foal. (I hope we can all agree that foals or mares with foals should not be in a pasture with a halter.) There is some merit in having to put a halter on and removing it as routine. It desensitizes the young horse to being bridled later on in training. There are also some exceptions to the "pasture" halter debate. For example, having more than one horse impacts the issue of halters. Being able to easily separate or sort the horses out allows me to reinforce the behavior patterns that keep them safe and establish a predictable routine—specifically having the same horse go out first, come in first, go to the wash stall first, and when safety is a priority, eating first. Halters allow this process to be easily instilled and corrected immediately if problems should arise and you do not have any extra help.

Several years ago, there were two adopted mustangs that came in to be boarded. These horses had never been touched by anyone. These two had been run through a corral chute into a stock trailer to travel to Virginia from a range in Wyoming. At some point, these horses were sedated, vaccinated, and fitted with nylon halters. The halters had an eight feet long piece of lead line attached. The halter and lead line was a drastic measure that we learned would be critical to the horses being able to be socialized and avoid a more dismal fate. It worked. The horses were confined to their stalls without being handled at all while being fed and watered through the stall enclosure. Eventually, we could enter the stall, touch their ropes, touch the horses, and the bonding process began. Coming in to direct contact with the head of a completely untrained horse would have been asking too much too soon. The halter training had to begin with these horses in a totally unconventional manner.

The other exception to wearing a halter is having the small lot area that is the focus of this work. My horses wear their halters when they are turned out. Again, they are visible in every area of the turn-out lots. The lots have been horse proofed, but the front yard and the adjoining roadway would not be safe if they managed to get out. In that circumstance, my level of anxiety and their heightened excitement would make catching them very risky. A halter in that instance would make the whole situation easier to resolve. It is for this reason that I feel having to replace two halters twice a year is worthwhile. (By the way, "breakaway" halters are not reliable. Horses could become entangled in any part of a headstall that comes off in the pasture, causing the very harm you are trying to prevent.)

Finally, my opinion is based on my experience and my situation. If my horses were out in a thirty-acre pasture, they would not be in a halter unless it was absolutely necessary for their safety or mine.

Next, the winter blanket argument is based more on science and less on individual opinion. First of all, horses like cold weather. Given the choice of shelter or exposure, most will opt to stay outside. We also know by observing their frisky, playful behavior on cold mornings. The problems occur when a horse is older, or bad weather sets in for a protracted period of time. When a horse is cold (check their ears), wet, and shivering, you have to get them inside—dried off, vigorously rubbed down, and into a heavy grade blanket. We have blankets for extreme weather and emergencies. You have to use a regional temperature chart to determine which weight and type is recommended for your area. There are stable blankets and turn-out rugs with a denier grade that varies based on the durability you desire. A blanket that is too heavy will make the horse sweat and actually make him colder. (Check for sweat by feeling up under the blanket in different areas.)

Make sure you take accurate measurements before ordering a blanket. (Measure from the middle of the chest around the point of the shoulder, straight across the horse's belly and hip around to mid tail. If your readings are not exact to suit the blanket size, choose the next size up.) As you look at blanket styles, choose one that is designed to lay either well above the withers or "cutback" from the withers to eliminate pressure on that area. The best blankets have a gusset feature over the front legs to prevent rubbing on the shoulders. Turn-out blankets have a tail cover for added warmth and protection, so that area should also be pressure free. My newest blanket has a belly-wrap feature that my horses seem to find comfortable with its added warmth. Remember to cross the belly surcingles, leaving a fist width of space for comfort. (Blankets are put on and secured front to back and removed back to front, always.) Pay close attention to the hind leg elastic straps. They tend to stretch out and need adjustment over time. Make sure there is not circumstance that they can get looped around the hock of the horse. If circumstances determine that you blanket your horse, make sure that you remove the blanket once a day, and do not neglect grooming. Again, check for sweating and remove the blanket if the horse is too warm. Turn-out blankets are the only type we use. In winter, when the footing is sloppy and it is too cold to bathe, the turn-out rug allows the horse-needed exercise. However, a horse left outside, in weather with the most expensive gear, is still subject to rain rot and all sorts of skin issues that you might not find until spring if you are negligent. They do not make a blanket that rain will not seep through around the withers and onto the back. A good winter blanket's insulating properties prevent the skin from drying out and inevitably skin problems occur.

In our mid-Atlantic climate, the consensus is that healthy horses do not need blankets. If you do not want to blanket, then start preparing the horse in midsummer. Do not body clip or expose the horse to excessive indoor lighting, which retards the natural growth of the winter coat that increases with the shorter days of fall.

Remember that an adequate natural coat, shelter from falling weather, enough forage, and adequate water will do more for your horse's winter health than an expensive blanket.

CHAPTER 12

Afterthoughts of Dreams and Memories

*God forbid that I should go to any
heaven in which there are no horses.*

—R. B. Cunningham Graham

If you are reading this book, you are most likely already a horse owner. It is my sincere hope that readers will find some useful advice and information to make the horse management process easier and less stressful. Perhaps, at the very least, this writing should assist you in knowing what questions to ask.

Those of you who do not have horses may be considering the prospect of buying your first horse. My main goal in this work was to encourage horse lovers to pursue your dream. The book reflects the reality that you do not have to be a large landowner or have an unlimited budget.

Do not wait as long as I did. I never owned a horse as a child. The horses that I worked with were lease horses from a riding camp in the North Carolinian mountains. They were "off-the-track" thoroughbreds that were retrained for hunt seat and jumping classes. (They wintered over on a farm outside the city limits of Lumberton.) In quick succession, I found myself riding and schooling a variety of quarter horses and saddlebreds. Fortunately, our Lumberton community had a large horse population, and my parents spent many hours driving me around to indulge my passion. These hours included my library trips to access every book on horses available.

My first horse was a pony named Dixie that we bought only after our young family moved to Caswell County. Shortly thereafter, a paint mare, a quarter horse colt, and four Arabians followed. Showing and trail riding with those horses make up some of my fondest memories.

Many highly regarded trainers have impacted my lifelong love of horses: Mr. Pete Lambeth and Linda Lambeth Watson of Davanna Stables; Ennis Hester of Bladenboro; Mitchell Wallace of Buchanan, VA; Maggie Gardner of Chatham, VA; and most recently, Eddie Tuck, whose name is very well-known at the Walking Horse Celebration in TN. (Eddie Tuck is the trainer who bred the two wonderful walking horses that are fulfilling my retirement years.) I have such a profound appreciation for you all. You have taught me by your fine example, your success, and your fine horses. I consider your influence a priceless gift.

Recommended Product Lists

Disclaimer: Please note that this list is a reflection of the supplies that I keep on hand for first aid and routine horse care. There are certainly many other comparable products, and you will, in time, develop your own list. These all perform as advertised and are readily available in most equine supply companies. Please always consult your veterinarian for product recommendations to ensure the best health outcome for your horse's unique needs.

Absorbine-Epsom salt	Soreness and swelling
Anti-itch gel	Any generic type
Benadryl cream	Itching
Banixx	All skin care products
Clorox	Bleach (for buckets and troughs)

Corona	Multipurpose (healing) ointment
Electrical tape	Heavy duty (for braiding)
Equiderma	Skin lotion for rain rot, ringworm, scratches, and sweet itch
Excalibur	Sheath, udder cleaner
Fung-a-Way	Topical antiseptic (spray)
Ivory soap	Sheath cleaning
Johnson's Baby Oil	Manes or tails
Kopertox	Thrush treatment
Oster Blade Wash	Clipper maintenance
Oster Kool Lube	Clipper maintenance
Purishield	Liquid bandage
Rainmaker	Hoof dressing
SWAT	Fly repellent for wounds
TRESemmé	Shampoo and conditioner (manes and tails and body)
TRI-Care	Wound treatment creme
Udder Butter	Soothing suave
UltraShield	Fly spray (absorbine)
Vaseline	Petroleum jelly (limits scarring and keeps scabs soft)
Vetrolin	Dry shampoo spray
Wahl Clippers	Cordless (for cosmetic trimming)
WD-40	Detangler
Wonder Dust	Blood coagulant (follow application directions)

(*Note:* It is recommended that you keep Banamine and bute on hand for horses with chronic pain issues. Your vet will advise you on their appropriate use on those occasions when you might need to begin treatment before they arrive.)

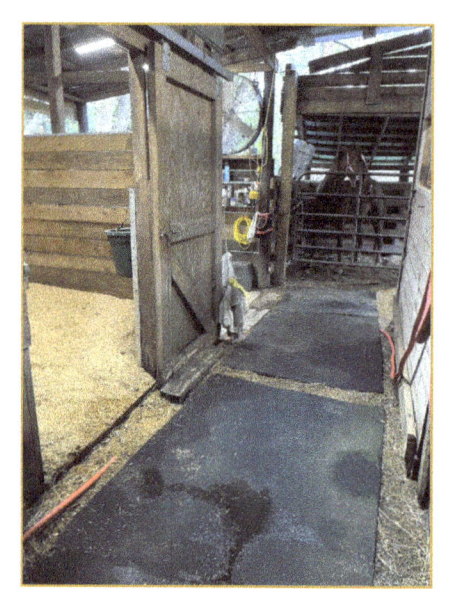

Main aisle - note narrow width to match rubber mats, and sliding stall door

Inside stall - note stall openings with bars and angle iron
*Bars are a safety feature needed for stalls in narrow aisles

HOME IS WHERE THE BARN IS

Pasture lane with four-rail fencing and truck access to hay room and riding ring

Dollar's stall with rough hewn boards, banked sawdust and hay in natural feeding position
*Hay nets can be safely used for trailering and medical situations where the horse's head has to be restrained

Feed room with secure metal barrels, storage, and electrical panels

SunKing at the Richmond Arabian Show

HOME IS WHERE THE BARN IS

SunKing at the Yanceyville Show in Open Pleasure Class

SunKing at Tightsqueeze, Virginia

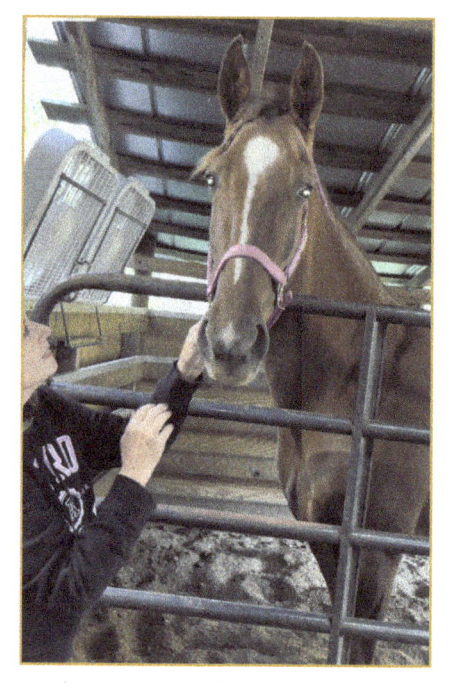

Skye inside open back shed with secure fan racks

SunKing at New London, Virginia

HOME IS WHERE THE BARN IS

Lighted wash stall with brushed cement floor and crosstie chains

Dollar and Skye inside back shed
*Access to the fans and inside lights make this turn-out shed more ideal than the more traditional stand alone structures that are found in many pastures

Dollar in backyard lot

Barn exterior- Feed room entrance to left and hay room double doors to the right

Dollar and Skye near barn lane entrance

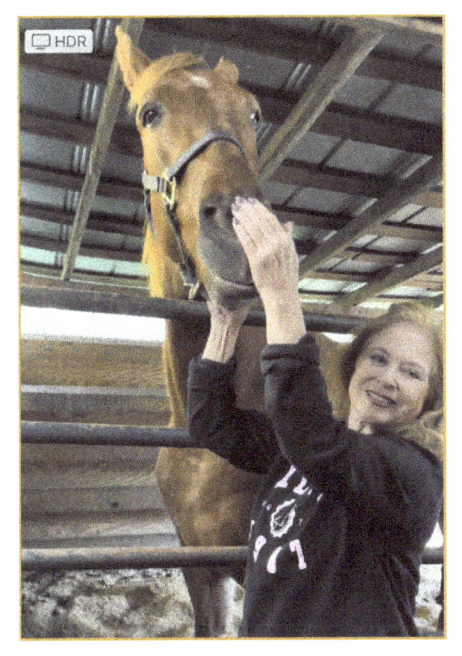

Dollar and the author

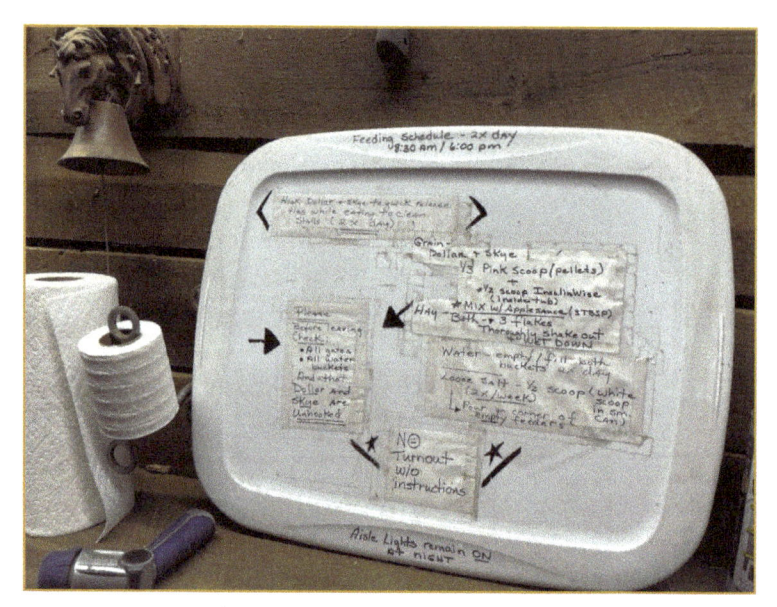

Feeding instructions on plastic tote lid

Dollar's finished 3-step braid secured with electric tape

WORKS CITED

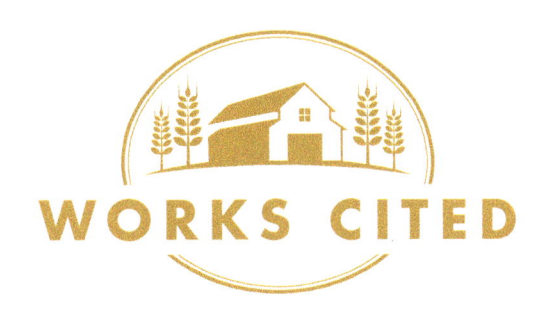

Blikslager, Anthony. July 26, 2018. *Avoiding Colic Through Management.* Arenus.com.

Carson, Deidre. et al. 2010. *Sweet Itch in Horses.* vcahospitals.com.

Duren, Stephen E. 2018. *Performance Horse Nutrition.* performancehorsenutrition.com.

Koontz, Robert H. 2021. *Equine Warts Papillomatosis.* CKEquineHospital.com.

Kristula, Michaela A. November 18, 2019. *Water Temperature and Horse Drinking Behavior.* thehorse.com.

McClure, Robert C. et al. 1993. *Functional Anatomy of the Horse Foot.* mospace.umsystem.edu.

Steffanus, Denise and Steve Norman. March 17, 2017. *What a Pain: Hoof Abscesses: A Common Frustration For Horses in All Life Stages.* paulickreport.com.

Young, Amy. March 23, 2020. *Laminitis.* UC Davis Veterinary Medicine Center for Equine Health. ceh,vetmed.ucdavis.edu.

ABOUT THE AUTHOR

Inspired by a variety of books on horses, the author's desire to own a horse began early. Her deep love of horses was encouraged by supportive parents who provided the opportunity to ride, school, and show horses for owners in the area. Southeastern North Carolina had many large horse farms and training facilities close by. Working directly with trainers of saddlebreds, thoroughbreds, and quarter horses provided a priceless in-depth equine education across three riding disciplines.

It was not until after college and the attainment of a graduate degree in the field of education that the goal of horse ownership was realized. The author's first "horse" was a pony named Dixie, large enough for an adult to ride and with a spirit generous enough to become a favorite family pet. Eight more horses have enriched life for the family.

Meanwhile, teaching provided for extensive travel in Europe and Asia—a series of thrilling adventures made even more so by seeing exotic foreign breeds of horses with their varied regional adaptations.

However, this author's favorite destination continues to be her home in Caswell County, North Carolina, near the Danville, Virginia, border, where her beloved horses share a small barn in her backyard.